FACING THE WALL

P9-CDX-420

FACING
THE
WALL

AMERICANS AT THE VIETNAM VETERANS MEMORIAL

Text by Duncan Spencer
Photographs by Lloyd Wolf

Collier Books   Macmillan Publishing Company
New York

Collier Macmillan Publishers
London

THE PHOTOGRAPHIC HISTORICAL SOCIETY
P.O. Box 39563, Rochester, N.Y. 14604
Visual Studies Workshop
Research Center
Rochester, N.Y.
June 22, 1987
Gift of the Publisher

Text copyright © 1986 by Duncan Spencer
Photographs copyright © 1986 by Lloyd Wolf

All rights reserved. No part of this book may be reproduced or transmitted in any form or by any means, electronic or mechanical, including photocopying, recording or by any information storage and retrieval system, without permission in writing from the Publisher.

Macmillan Publishing Company
866 Third Avenue, New York, N.Y. 10022
Collier Macmillan Canada, Inc.

Library of Congress Cataloging-in-Publication Data
Spencer, Duncan.
    Facing the wall.
    1. Vietnamese Conflict, 1961–1975—Personal narratives, American.   2. Veterans—United States—Biography.   3. Vietnam Veterans Memorial (Washington, D.C.)   I. Wolf, Lloyd.   II. Title.   III. Title: Americans at the Vietnam Veterans Memorial.
DS559.5.S64   1986   959.704'38   86-4214
ISBN 0-02-096880-9

Macmillan books are available at special discounts for bulk purchases for sales promotions, premiums, fund-raising, or educational use. For details, contact:

Special Sales Director
Macmillan Publishing Company
866 Third Avenue
New York, N.Y. 10022

10 9 8 7 6 5 4 3 2 1
PRINTED IN THE UNITED STATES OF AMERICA

Design by Antler & Baldwin, Inc.

Facing the Wall is also published in a hardcover edition by Macmillan Publishing Company.

Acknowledgments

Thanks to Sandra Alley and Steve Alemar of the National Capital Parks Service, Bill Schoendorf, Peter Deer, and Sara Schaeffer. Lloyd is grateful to those who directly assisted him—Stephanie Gross, Jennifer Murphy, and especially Alice Welsh. We would also like to thank our families for their patience and support.

Dedicated to Tom Hardy, to Tom Marsden, and to my students

PREFACE

"Sometimes I think that maybe I'm a war criminal." He spoke casually, but carefully. It was half a joke, half a confession. I hadn't thought about either the war or him for ten years. In 1973 I was working with a recently returned Vietnam veteran. Multiple tours. An officer in the Rangers—the army's best. A strapping Clark Kent of a man, raised on a Pennsylvania farm. All-American, he went to war sincerely believing he was fighting to preserve the American ideals of democracy and freedom. From what I understand, he fought hard, and he fought well. I'm certain he was an exceptional soldier. He came home to a divided and unreceptive country. He questioned his service, his actions, the government's motives in sending him there. His confusion about his role was obvious. He wanted to go to medical school and go back to Vietnam as a doctor, to help heal a country he felt he had helped tear apart. Last I heard, he didn't get in. A very decent man, a good man to work for. I lost touch with him. I wonder about him and what peace he has made for himself. Life continues.

Nineteen fifty-nine to 1975. American military involvement in Vietnam— The War—started when I was in first grade and ended after I left college. It was Big Time Hot from sixth grade on.

In 1974 my supervisor at work had fairly recently been released from an eighteen-month prison term for resisting the draft. A pleasant, ordinary, down-to-earth guy. He handled the phones, dealt with clients, dispatched our courier, did some production work. Happily married, he has three kids now. I remember him being visited by fellow resisters with whom he had done time. I remember him getting a letter offering limited and conditional amnesty to war resisters, issued by President Ford. I saw him angrily fold it up at his desk, grumbling and cursing for a minute before he went back to work. I remember him saying that he thought it might have been easier and better if he had just let himself get drafted and get it over with. Jail was a drag—eighteen months out of his life, ripped away and ripped off. He almost never talked about it. He wanted life to go on, as normal as life gets. Like many of the veterans, he was swept into the whirlpool of the Vietnam War. Difficult decisions had to be made at a young age. Ten years later, he doesn't want to dwell on the past. Life continues.

I hadn't dealt with thoughts of the war myself for ten years. I had friends and colleagues who were veterans, peace activists, or relatives of the same. I half forgot that my father was in Saigon in 1968 as a civilian technical advisor working for the United States Navy during the crucial explosion of the Tet offensive. I watched the community I live in fill up with Indochinese refugees, but didn't think about it too deeply. Vietnam was pushed out of my consciousness as too painful, as something best left behind. The rest of the country also seemed to undergo this same process. I thought, and perhaps we all thought, don't dwell on this mess, life continues. Get on with it.

Neither a person nor a nation can ever really shrug off its past. These photographs and these interviews are an attempt to tell the human side of the American involvement in Vietnam. The Vietnam Memorial in Washington, D.C., draws millions of visitors each year. Although many experience it as tourists, many have more powerful reasons for going there. I have attempted to make as honest a picture of each person we interviewed as I could.

In general the pictures were made quickly. In most cases I only asked the people to "please look this way." Everyone interviewed agreed to have their picture made, and they were aware of being photographed. Photographing them was my way of coming to grips with them and the aspect of their lives that was tied up in the war or the memorial. Within the limits of my abilities and of the medium I have tried to be truthful to them. I tried to avoid the most obvious manipulations and artifices available to me. I don't believe there is really such a thing as "a good straight photograph," but I have tried to make them nonetheless. All photographs have an inherent subjective and fictional quality—they are taken by people, and in themselves are not real. But, like maps, photographs can provide a pretty accurate description and guide to perceiving the real world. These photographs and interviews are, I hope, roughly accurate descriptions of these people at this wall. They are a map of each person—a personal map created by the interchange between these people and myself. Take whatever highways you find into their lives and faces.

Being at the wall for over a year has transformed me. It is a powerful place. It contains one full football stadium of dead men's and women's names. People. And the living come to reflect, to reexperience, to remember. I have become more aware of the trials and strengths of the human spirit. I have become partially numbed by shocking stories. I have become more aware of the human side of war. I have thought a long time about the word *sacrifice*. I have looked closely at and paid attention to these particular people. I have thought about Vietnam—the war, its dead, and its survivors. For the survivors, like it or not, with terror and with grace and at this moment, life continues.

Lloyd Wolf
May 1986

INTRODUCTION

By the end of 1979 the melancholy statistic was circulating in the Veteran's Administration that more than 60,000 men who had served in the armed forces during the Vietnam era had committed suicide. So the number of men killed by the enemy was less than that of the suicides.

These figures are a shock, yet like so many things about the war, they are an illusion: considering the number that served—over six million—the suicide rate is close to normal.

Over 58,000 men and women were killed in combat during our fifteen years in Vietnam. Yet these figures, too, are an illusion, exceeded in a single morning in the trenches of World War I.

But Vietnam was and forever will be different. The disastrous outcome of the war, the inequalities of the draft, the class and racial antagonisms it spawned, as well as the apparently permanent distrust of government action, are sad proofs of that.

The unease and confusion and loss in this country have not ended, but future decades may date the beginning of a new outlook from the unveiling of a long-delayed monument to the Vietnam War dead in 1982. It was the result of a single man, Jan C. Scruggs, a not particularly distinguished veteran of the war who at a vital moment told those gathered at a meeting in Washington that there should be such a monument.

Other suggestions put forward at that meeting included scholarships and more legislation to help the survivors of the war and their unique hardships. For a tribute to the fallen, the planting of trees was suggested, perhaps a memorial grove. Scruggs alone spoke of a monument, and he insisted from the beginning that it have two characteristics: that it list the names of everyone who died, and that it be paid for, not by the government, but by individual Americans.

But not even Scruggs could have foreseen that the wall would become one of the most visited monuments in Washington. It was not planned to be so, for unlike most war memorials it was not a civic project but a private one, financed by veterans themselves in a dramatic rebuke to a nation they felt had scorned them. Scruggs's committee of veterans sponsored a nationwide contest for a design for the memorial. To ensure objectivity, all submissions were considered blindly, without names. The winning entry was striking: a stark black marble slab, set directly into the earth. Its designer was a young woman, Oriental, who was not even an architect when, as a student at Yale Architecture School, she submitted her plan. Maya Lin had been a child when the war was claiming most of its victims.

From the first, the plans for the somber black cliff drew controversy. Orthodox war memorials display flags, striving men, generals on prancing horses, the classical symbols of national pride, honor, glory. This one spoke only of death and loss. A deep split was revealed in the ranks of the Vietnam War veterans; there were those who thought the Lin design—an open and accepting form rather than a thrusting and heroic pillar—was somehow a political statement. The design was lashed as a "black gash of shame" in newspapers, and Scruggs's fund-raising group, the Vietnam Memorial Fund, was criticized in an investigative television series.

The pressure for a more "heroic" image for the men who fought in Vietnam resulted in the Frederick Hart statue, the Three Fighting Men, which was placed facing the wall at a distance and was given the blessing of a visit from President Ronald Reagan, who had previously distanced himself from the memorial project.

From the beginning, the men and women who worked on the Vietnam Veterans Memorial had not foreseen its almost mystical pull. The public seemed disinclined, when the monument was finished, to be reminded of the war. Veterans of the war were the subjects of an uncomfortable pity or, worse, suspected of mass psychosis.

But the paths and the sward alongside the memorial told a different story. As access areas were worn down and trampled again and again, and the fresh sod so quickly ruined, observers knew they were viewing an inarticulate phenomenon.

Night lighting of the wall became necessary because people did not stop at dusk but came with their flashlights and candles when the wall was quieter and more private. The expensive illumination, which casts an eerie glow from ground level upward onto faces and names, made the marble slabs look like altars.

As visitors filed past in greater and greater numbers, it became clear that the memorial, by chance or design, had at last presented an acceptable image of the nation's experience and its reaction to Vietnam. The image was of an America chastened, in mourning, but directly facing the reality of waste and death. It was as direct as the names themselves, coming into view like a silenced host, first as a blur of lines and then in crystal clarity, without military rank, without personal history, without even the line between officers and enlisted men. Only the chronology of death—for each name is closest to those who died at the same time.

The interviews and photographs that make up this book were taken over a period of more than a year, from the spring of 1984 to the late summer of 1985. The authors attempted to approach a cross section of the thousands of people who come to the memorial, knowing that it is not only the ex-soldiers who have been affected by Vietnam, but also their families, their friends, their neighbors—the ones who have so seldom found *their* stories told.

For the wall is an intensely public place. There you will hear kids callously joking about finding their own names carved into the panels and, a few feet away, a veteran or a father weeping inconsolably; you will hear a tourist asking whether the bodies are buried here, too. You may see a veteran lay down a medal and a youth pick it up and pocket it a few minutes later. You will hear the stories of death, of valor, of bragging—and of mental collapse and madness. You will find a stream of humanity, most indifferent, some merely curious, a few transfixed by memory and emotion.

The stories of *Facing the Wall* were taped or taken down by hand. Nothing was added to the words spoken, but much was taken away to form a tighter sequence of thoughts. The place, with its almost hysterical focus on death, seems to elicit memories long held back, just as the names themselves bring the faces of the dead to the mirror of the mind.

Larry Neil White

Larry Neil White is thirty-three and round like a baby, though his eyes are too quick, never resting, and the wrinkles around them are deeper than they should be. Altogether his compact figure is a portrait of unease, like a powerful little bear in chains. He came to the wall from Owensboro, Kentucky, in the western part of the state, the dark tobacco country, where he now lives.

I'd never been to the nation's capital, so I wanted to come here for that reason, and I wanted to see the fireworks, and I got the idea of bringing the Kentucky state flag here because a friend of mine had said there wasn't a Kentucky flag there at the memorial.

Can you believe those suckers charged me twenty-six dollars for a state flag? I had gone to the capital to get one, there in Louisville, and I told this guy, "You got about as much patriotism as a rock," but I still had to pay. I went to the office of my state representative, that's Delbert Murphy, and he was too embarrassed to ask me for the twenty-six dollars. Still had to pay it though.

I felt like if I didn't do this, take this upon myself to get our flag here, it wouldn't be done. I knew of nineteen other states which have sent delegations, they told me that at Louisville, at the veterans outreach center. That's where I got the idea.

So I went to the wall last night at midnight with my state flag, the one my state senator got me, and I was there from midnight to 9:30, when a little Park Ranger told me I have to leave. I was standing at the apex there, and there were three guys from Owens-

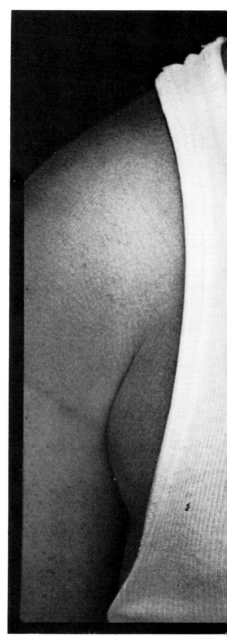

boro there with me. We had the idea of doing this vigil, and this little son of a bitch comes up and tells me I've got to go and I've been there for seven, eight hours while nobody bothers. There was an altercation with this Park Ranger and he said we had threatened him and he called us a "bunch of crazy bastards" and he went for the supervisor, and when *he* came I told him, "Nobody told me I was crazy when I was in Vietnam." Then I went off and took some of my medicine, Tofranil, a mood elevator; I take three tranquilizers now, Xanax, which is a leveler, and Desyrel, which is a controller.

I wanted to hit that man with my flagpole, real bad. He didn't say Larry White was a crazy man per se, he said all these shits is crazy, and I said, "Are you calling me crazy? I don't have to take this—what's your name, I want to talk to your supervisor." I demanded an apology.

Owensboro's just a one-dog town. If there's any more than one dog, they've got a dog problem. In the service, I thought, I can do what I want to do. The recruiter, he showed me a film of these tanks. I liked it. I wanted to ride. If I was going to go, I wanted to ride. It was the Sheridan tank, the first tank with a computer. We went to leadership prep school and fourteen months after I was a civilian farm boy I was the commander of an eighteen-and-a-half ton tank. I liked the army fine and after the first eighteen months I reenlisted for six years. Well, you know how I got that Silver Star?

It was in the Ashau Valley near Khesanh; the unit was about sixty people, three tanks, four armored personnel carriers, a mortar APC. We were loggerheaded up for the night, command center in the middle and all the vehicles pointed out on a hilltop, what they called a NDP or night defense perimeter. There are four guys in each tank, the commander, the gunner, the loader, the driver.

It was dark night, 11:00 P.M., and I was sleeping outside, and the first thing I knew, the gooks hit us with mortars. I hollered, ran to the tank and I could hear someone's fifty going. Things didn't look too bad until they started firing the RPGs [rocket-propelled grenades], and right away I knew that one of them was going to hit us. I was sitting in the hatch

with the loader and the damn thing came right through the side of the tank and I could look down past my leg into the tank and see this thing ricochet like a red-hot bee around inside. It took the gunner's leg off and it killed the loader. The second rocket came in under the coaxial machine gun. We had a beehive, which is antipersonnel, just throws out thousands of bullets called flechettes; naturally the beehive had to be electronically loaded. I was thinking my vehicle is pretty well wrecked—the only thing still working was the machine gun, and we fired about nine thousand rounds, melting a barrel. The driver ran into a mortar pit and I never saw him until it was over. Then the gooks were inside the wire and we were dusting them off just as they were demo'ing the tank, and killed both rocket crews, which is why I was put in for the Silver Star.

Everything was all right after that, but I started getting in trouble. I came back from the war and was stationed at Fort Knox. My first wife had already left me.

In all, I've been married five times, and that was the first. It was Cynthia left me while I was in Vietnam, and then there was Angela, she was a college student, she went back to Connecticut after I was arrested for intoxication. I was into drugs and alcohol. Laura Jean left me after nineteen months—drinking and drugs—I thought I was the only one knew where I was at. I went to the G.I. bill and took a two-year nursing program. I ended up marrying the head nurse there after fourteen months; Rebecca, that was her name, and I warned her (she was a good Christian girl, she went to church every time the doors was open) so that after a year and a half, she said to herself, "Hey, this motherf—— ain't *going* to change."

I went off and started two different businesses, dropped out of school and went to vocational school—there was just no continuity to my life. After Rebecca I finally took a job as a security guard, it was plant security at an aluminum plant, and damned if I didn't get rapid promotion, maybe it was I was looking for the army all over again; I got special assignments, and at one point I was guarding Kris Kristofferson and Rita Coolidge while they were on tour in Alabama in 1979.

This time I stayed single for about two-and-a-half years and married this old girl in Alabama, and I stayed married to her for about nineteen to twenty months. Then I was off doing a security job in some old redneck town, Muscle Shoals, it must have been, and when I went back to Birmingham I found my wife had left with everything but the carpet.

Then I got a job at Hill Air Force Base in Utah at the Ogden Air Logistics Command, and when I had worked there for exactly one year and three days, Mr. Kent, the supervisor of my boss, said there was something wrong with my application to work. I threw my application and I threw my I.D. at him.

I sold my car, sold my waterbed, took out all my savings, and I got about four thousand dollars together and I went for a month to Hawaii. Laying on the beach, smoking Kona gold at two hundred dollars an ounce, it doesn't take long to run through your pile.

In June of '82, I hadn't visited with my folks in six years, and when I left, I wasn't getting along with my dad. They said they had a little rental house I could stay [in] in Owensboro. They even offered to come out to Salt Lake to pick me up. They charged me only $150 per month. And there was this lady next door, very pretty, with two teen-aged daughters. I was going to a heavy combat rap group, I started going back and forth to Louisville. I promised Jo-Ann, I told her, "I know I'm sick, but if you'll marry me. . . ." Well, she married me and I'm still with her. She takes care of me, she makes sure I take my medicine. I could never handle money. She takes it all and gives me fifty dollars a week for cigarettes. She takes my money and buys the groceries and pays the bills. She's hung in there with me.

One time I had a flashback. It was at a banquet and I had drunk some. I heard 'copters, gunfire. I grabbed her and pushed her face into a brick wall; blacked both her eyes and gave her a concussion. I was so sorry when I'd found out what I had done. I checked into a VA hospital and from the time I started to when I ended I spent 167 days in that hospital.

After I did that to Jo-Ann I had to give up my drink. I had my last drink October 1, 1983, with a bottle of Jack Daniels, and I laid that bottle down and I said never again.

I think I've spent ten years in a trancelike state, and I'm tired of having these nightmares. For the first time in my life, I'm doing something productive. My wife drives a new car, it seems like a miracle finally happening.

I got a lawyer on my case and I finally got my 100 percent disability this February. That's two thousand dollars each month. They gave me 60 percent in '82, 40 percent in '78, and 30 percent in '74, and I kept appealing it. I knew I had this post-traumatic stress syndrome. What does it mean? Over the years I have had a real difficult time dealing with people, I have a violent temper. I've held thirty-nine jobs in ten years—dishwasher, working on a riverboat, truck driver, even the exterminating business. I've been in jail twenty-seven times and married five times. I've made threats on persons, and I've assaulted a police officer.

Since I've been involved with these vets, there's been a newspaper story about me in Owensboro. I was getting a lot of satisfaction out of it. I bought a van and started giving disabled vets rides to the hospital and other places and within three months, with the help of this VFW post I got two cars and two vans and eleven guys helping me, and I spent about six thousand dollars out of my own pocket. Jo-Ann says, "Hey, sucker, slow down."

So that's how I got to the monument. We got here Sunday and we're staying until Friday. I've visited the White House and the Vietnam Memorial and I'm staying in Virginia. I knew I was coming and I knew I was going to bring that flag up here if I had to do it myself.

To me, it means America. To see all those names, all those dead boys, or kids. I was only nineteen when I went over there. I got here the first time, I just sat down and I cried, and we cried and we held each other. Them old beer-bellied dudes, I'm proud of them.

All those dead boys; I feel that by seeing their names in granite I can lay some of these ghosts.

John Sumida

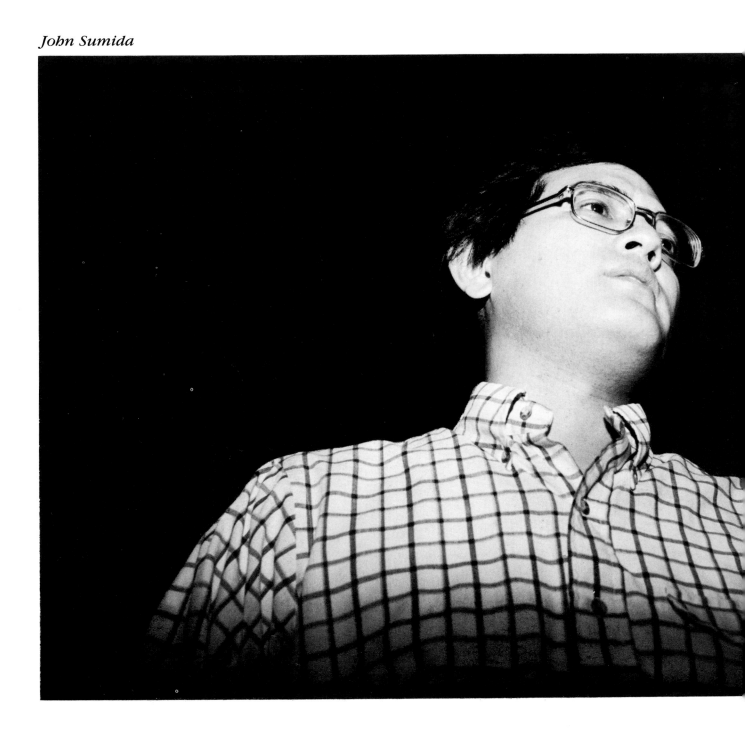

Mild exterior, scholarly manner, and an intellectual's penchant for linking events all mask John Sumida's iron will. A Japanese-American, he was brought up with the concept of duty to country, the son of one of the famed Nisei who fought for the United States in World War II and proved their loyalty with horrific casualties. He went to jail rather than submit to the Vietnam draft. He is a military historian, now teaching at the University of Maryland. He served eighteen months in prison in the mid-1970s.

My teacher cut out a Vietnam Day poster, I can remember it very clearly; it was my first memory of the war, sophomore year in high school, 1963. I was always a current events buff, and soon I had a map of Vietnam on the wall with flags. By senior year I was prowar, I remember.

My parents, like so many Japanese-Americans, were very quiet. They were analytical about their World War II experience—my grandfather's business was destroyed, my father was a Nisei. But their attitude towards Vietnam was less important than their attitude toward military service—a belief that serving in the army was the right course. I had uncles in the 442d, the famous Japanese unit. The idea that you should serve even if the government is doing wrong was a very important part of the family.

By sophomore year in college, I had become mildly antiwar. I was one of the leaders of minority students at the University of California. Part of a group who viewed the war as an imperialist war. I decided, by junior year, that I would finesse the whole war thing by enlisting and opt to go to language school in Russian.

But then I had a lottery number which was not impossibly high, so that in '71 I was draft-eligible. What changed my mind was the invasion of Cambodia. What I felt disturbed about was that Nixon and Kissinger were doing things when the president had said we weren't. The electorate was being asked to accept behavior by the executive, allow it and legitimize it. I didn't believe in conscientious-objector status—it seemed like that was cutting a deal with the government. I knew, for example, that none of my white friends were going to war. Four hundred dollars and a lawyer could stretch out the time almost indefinitely. There were doctors, there were deferments. The other in my decision to resist was the speaker who urged people to turn in their draft cards—and after the speech I asked him if he had turned his in and he said no.

From that point on I decided to resist. I would say no at each stage of the procedure. I had already foreseen that there were times that the only correct place to be was in prison.

One of the things which made me turn to personal direct action was that I was tired of radical politics, group actions, radical actions I found hard to support.

When I went to my physical, at every point where I was asked a question, I said no. I was notified I was one-A in the draft sometime after. In the fall of '71 I refused induction, and after refusal, I received notice I would be prosecuted. I went through two trials—at the first one there was a hung jury. My defense was not that the war was illegal—we knew that would not work. My lawyer and his assistant and I scoured the literature and we held that a "reasonable man" would believe that the war was illegal or unconstitutional. Ironically, it was a military man on the jury who refused to go for the guilty. The next trial we lost hands down. Two years.

I was not clear then and I am not clear now about why one does go to jail. Sometimes people do things just to define themselves. There was a sense that I would serve a year, or perhaps six months. I thought if I couldn't serve eighteen months and come out in reasonable shape I couldn't take anything and I better find this out.

I had a good education. I thought of things systematically, made an analysis of the war, selected the right course. Now, could I do it? I thought I could. The financial situation was okay. There would be career damage. I wasn't married, I had no kids, it was my decision, my life. It was essential to my development as a scholar—if ideas have meaning—to do all this and punt it, it would have been a signal not to be a historian.

Prison was not a waste of time. I practiced the trumpet four or five hours a day and read extremely widely. There were a few draft evaders, ten dope dealers, ten racketeers, and a few blacks. I was regarded as an American Indian. One of the Indians asked me what tribe I was in! They were so sure that a while later he came back and said, "Look, we'll tell the others you're a member of one of the eastern tribes."

By the time I was in prison, it was good to be a draft resister because of

Watergate. I felt distinctly lucky; for after Watergate it was very difficult to deny parole for draft resisters—the parole officer was a black, and I can't tell you why, but I was lucky. He asked me questions about my rehabilitation, questions about what I would do if I had the choice again. I said I would do the same thing and he smiled at that.

Prison was *not* bad for me. There was a lot of stress—I'll tell you, when some guy wants to assault you. But in my case the black cons put an end to this. People (middle-class people that is) think that when you are attacked, you become passive. So long as you make it clear that you don't care what happens to you—that you'll do anything to prevent *it* happening—it won't.

Within this framework, which is at least a framework of law, it was worth it, for if you weren't willing to do eighteen months, what were you willing to do? What I was offered by the draft system was the chance to make a statement. As I told the judge, this was a case on which honorable men could have a disagreement.

Jerry Lucero

Jerry Lucero rode up from Lubbock, Texas, in a rented car with a small group of veteran friends, all Spanish-Americans, all members of the South Plains Vietnam Vets Association. He got through the war as a marine grunt, but far from unscathed. His worst wounds he got coming home.

The worst thing that happened to me in the war happened in the Los Angeles airport. I was going home on leave—I got wounded in 1967—we were under fire while trying to take a wounded man back and my gas mask got hung up. But it wasn't a bad wound.

In the airport I was making a phone call with a friend. I was talking with my mother, and this other guy—he's from San Antonio—was talking on the next phone and shots rang out and the guy right next to me was killed. This crazy guy gets arrested. He was shouting we didn't deserve to be back—we were murderers. Both our mothers heard that shot and I had to pick up the phone and tell his mother what happened. I escorted his body home to San Antonio. I found out he never even got a scratch in Vietnam. I tried to shut the whole thing out of my mind.

I work in drug prevention, I am working with kids. There is a nonprofit organization—me and three other guys started ten years ago working with kids and vets. One kid asked me if I was really in the U.S. Marine Corps because he wanted to become a marine. I told him I never wore my uniform again after the airport. But I was proud.

Robert Muller

Robert Muller is the president of the Vietnam Veterans of America, the largest single organization for vets of that war. Born of Swiss parents, he shared many immigrants' reverence for an adopted country. Both scholar and athlete in school and college, he fit the mold of the all-American boy, even to his enlistment in the Marine Corps, where he so excelled that he was at the top of his class. He gladly went off to war as a second lieutenant in September 1968 with the Third Marine Division. Next April 29 his unit was assigned to take an obscure hill, and that changed his whole life.

They told us line officers we were running eighty-five percent casualties. We talked a lot about it. I remember, being the athlete I was—I remember with such conviction saying that if I lost a leg in Vietnam I would ask the nearest man to put a bullet to my head. To keep things calm at home, I told everyone that I was a supply officer. I guess I got shot because I was reckless. I was with ten tanks, eight guns, and two flamethrowers and we had run into this hill with a suicide squad of North Vietnamese Army soldiers. My group was ARVN [Army of the Republic of Vietnam] soldiers. They just would not sustain an attack on the enemy. Every time we got into combat, all three of our ARVN units tried to run.

So we called for four jet strikes to drop their whole payload on this little hill—plus a half hour heavy bombardment. Eight gun tanks blasted it with high explosive and flechette rounds. One tank burned the f—— hill and the tank commanders said they could see these guys bleeding in the head from the concussion.

There was a colonel in a helicopter on my case. "Take the goddamn hill." With three tanks, I got behind the lead tank and as we were walking up a guy comes out of a hole, and I dinged him—as best as I can figure it out, it was his partner who dinged me. It was one shot. It went through both lungs and exited, severing the spinal cord.

It was an Australian dragged me off the hill. With my luck, the hospital ship *Repose* was right off the coast near Quangtri, and I was told if I had arrived one minute later, I would have been dead.

After I was shot, I was conscious for thirty or forty-five seconds, long enough to know I was hit. My first thought was my girl—"She's going to kill me! Number two, I'm not going to worry about that because I'm going to die here on this stinking hill."

I can only describe it as being in the middle of a kaleidoscope—that must have been the spinal—and after that no feeling of pain but a mellow and relaxed feeling. I was looking up at the sky and getting a very warm, mellow sensation, it was like a balloon deflating. I felt life ebbing away. You can't grab it and you can't stop it. That's it. I think when you are mortally wounded you know it. I said to myself, "I don't believe it, I'm gonna die on this shitty piece of ground"—and I wake up on a hospital ship and everything was over.

On the ship I couldn't believe I was alive. People say there are those who grieve over their loss. I was just stunned that I was alive. I was euphoric. The thought never entered my mind that I was not going to make it. They told me right there the likelihood that I was going to be paralyzed. I told them that's okay, I was so f—— happy to be alive and for my entire life from that moment I have never looked at myself for what I have lost but for what I have got. Life is all a gift.

Even on the hospital ship the doctors said how lucky I was to be going to Kingsbridge Hospital in New York, but the first day I went from the naval hospital to the Veterans Administration hospital was the first day I cried.

It was physically dilapidated, depressing, run down. It stunk of urine and was filled with old guys who had no place to go. To come from the navy to this! Ironically, because of the war there had been cutbacks for the VA. The hospital was overcrowded and understaffed, but worse than that, it didn't have any spark, it didn't have any drive. It was a geriatric care facility. They say the May 20, 1970, issue of *Life* magazine was the second-largest-selling issue. The cover story was on my ward. There were close to ninety patients in three different wards, most of them paraplegic, and since I was the only college graduate I became the mouthpiece.

Ultimately, the VA did rehab the ward because of this: hell, ultimately they tore down the whole freaking hospital. But my closest friend in the hospital killed himself two or three years after. There are a fair number of suicides in the spinal wards. We came up with eight guys who were suicides. When guys have single-car accidents at ninety miles an hour on the center span of some bridge, you think, well. . . .

The most important thing for me out of this whole trip was the traumatic realization that life is a finite process. Everyone knows you die, but you put it out of your mind. This does tend to make some things important and others unimportant.

Jason Daly

I'm pretty sure my father was in Vietnam—or some . . . yeah, I'm pretty sure it was Vietnam. He's forty-four.

Yesterday, we went up to Arlington, and seeing a wreath-laying ceremony was really touching. I cried because it was such a feeling inside. Why they had to . . . I don't know, but seeing all the graves and, it's sad but it's. . . . Vietnam is not deep history, it's pretty present, but I've never really talked about it. We don't study it in school, and I wish we would more, though.

It would be nice to have something here like they have up at the Tomb [of the Unknowns]. Not glorious, but more honorable. Like maybe a guard or something, that would be nice because I was really impressed with that. And being out there [the Vietnam Veterans Memorial], it's nice, but it needs more honor, I think. Because these are men who died for their country.

No, I can't even say that; I mean, they died for somebody else.

Nancy Friedson

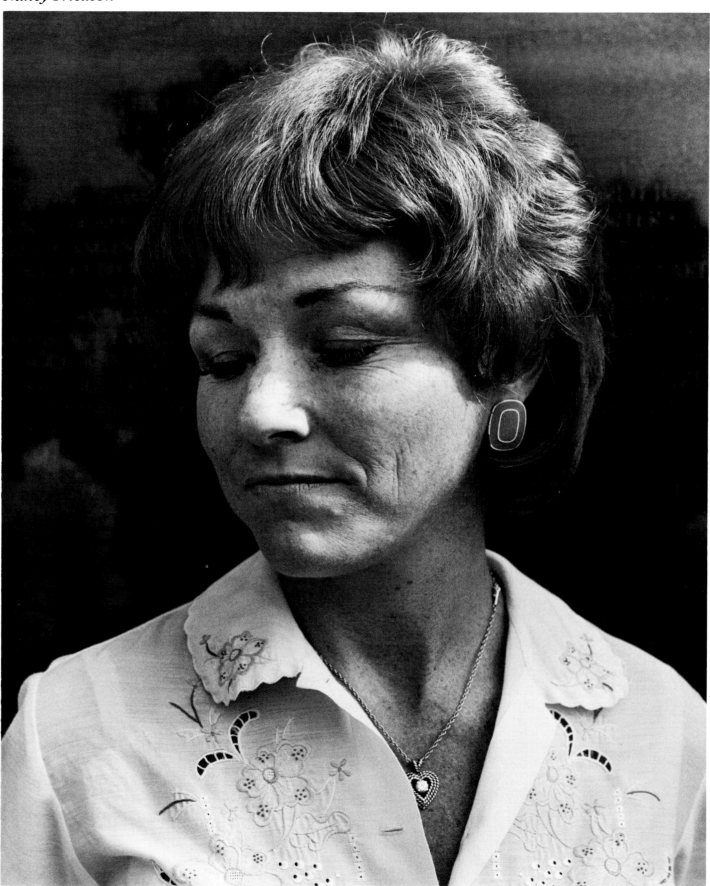

Somewhere along the line I saw one touching picture or heard one touching story that made me want to come here. All those names, all those stories, all those lives on one simple cut in the earth . . . I don't know how to explain it. I was very glad I came by myself.

In the late sixties I started flying for Pan Am. I did a lot of R & Rs. Camranh Bay and Danang and Saigon and taking the soldiers for their R & R, and I remember just how unaware we were . . . as flight attendants, we knew there was a war going on, but we had no real awareness of what these guys were going through, and all we knew at our servicing level was that we wanted to . . . kind of get their mind off what it was that they were experiencing.

So we'd do stupid things like when we were doing the lifejacket demonstrations, we'd cut out Playboy bunnies and tape them to the overhead box flap so that when we'd pull the thing down like this there'd be a little nude girl on it; we were always doing things like this. And the guys got a big kick out of that, but when I look at that wall I think, my God! They were in a whole different world! How could they even find humor in that or in anything. I was twenty-two.

Those flights were very different. There was a profound difference in taking them from Vietnam for their R & R and bringing them back after their R & R . . . for one thing, and this had nothing to do with the military, they were the best passengers in the world, because they're so used to doing what they're told that they file in like they're supposed to and they sit down, and they're so appreciative, and they . . . I seem to remember it wasn't like one big party the moment they were leaving Vietnam, some of them seemed in a . . . a lot of them were still very quiet and somber. Definitely coming back you could have heard a pin drop.

We took a lot of them to Hong Kong and Bangkok. It was joshing around. I don't remember any serious talks with them. I think they didn't want that at all. Now, I think if I had that kind of flight again, I would welcome an opportunity to talk to them or have them talk to me—to share their experience. But maybe then, my age then, my inexperience—I was just a kid—but I don't remember any of us having serious talks, or these guys wanting to have serious talks. They just wanted to be out of there.

I had a boyfriend—he was injured over there as a helicopter pilot. He had a bullet that went through the helicopter and went up into his foot and through his foot and up into . . . but he said his reaction to that was he was just furious when he found out he was injured. He wasn't so much in pain as just—angry—how dare they! He didn't even know until he'd taken off his boot.

The little impression about it I got from him was that our boys were sent there and were not allowed to do the job they were sent for. He was always saying it was like he had at least one hand tied behind him—that we could have knocked out that country in one day if we had to.

Roger and Kathy Williamson

Unlike other Vietnam marriages, the Williamsons, Roger and Kathy, kept breaking up and regrouping. They married before the war; Roger came back a changed man—troubled, unable to keep his job as a tool cutter. She hung on for sixteen years, and now they face life together. He came to the wall from Arkansas.

In Vietnam it was simple. There wasn't any black, white, green, yellow—you just made up your mind that this was what you were going to do for 365 days of your life. You were together. But back here, everyone had the gimmies—"me, me, me." Over there, it was "us, us, us, and let's get out of here."

Maybe I can put it to rest here. To be with people who have been through the same conditions, experiences, places—it's sixteen years. It's time to put it to bed.

I have been sleeping with it long enough. It's just me coming here to this place, letting my feelings go, letting go with the rest of the sorrow and the death. It'll always be with me but I want to leave the part that's gnawing at me always. Just leave that part.

John Shaughnessy

John Shaughnessy married a woman who was a war protester and thought veterans were psychotics. He laughed at the time, but he found that he simply could not hold back the anger. He was driven by recurring dreams to seek counseling. Intensely controlled, he now holds a high-paying job. He was a door gunner in a helicopter.

It's not gonna go away. There's nothing I can do about it. There's no way I can change what I've done. I can't change what I've seen. My nightmares are now an accepted part of life. And that's the way it is.

It's like being a cripple. You can't change being a cripple, but you can learn to deal with it, you can learn to live with it, you can look at it every day in the mirror and say it's here.

Vietnam: I went over there to be in military intelligence; I ended up as a door gunner in a helicopter. I was all over. The Delta to Phu Bai. I got to carry secret documents and to shoot people too—what a great deal. I'm still absolutely lucky to be alive. I mean I don't gamble now, I don't ski now, I don't do any high-risk activity, because my luck has run out! Over there it was, well, thirty-five seconds after the shooting started there was a 90 percent chance you were going to be dead. You're a wide-open target. You're sitting in a wide-open door with nowhere to go. All you can do is to try to return the body of the fire. . . .

I know friends who were over there in '68, '69, they're gone, they're wasted, they're crazy. They've got the two-thousand-yard stare. The Veterans Administration: I made every last goddam dime myself. I didn't like that f——— "help." They didn't help me before, they aren't gonna help me now. They can die up there, those bureaucrats.

This country's never said, "What you did was all right. We know that what you did, you did to survive." They never said that. They start saying it now— fourteen years too late!

You know, my parents never, to this day, asked me about Vietnam. Two years ago, my wife brought it up, and my dad didn't know I was in combat. They never asked, I never told.

Each person has to decide for himself how he's going to deal with it. These people here, walking up and down in front of the monument, they're never going to come up to these guys and say, "It's okay what you did. We understand." They're not going to say that, because they don't care! They don't f——— care! All these things are to them are *names*. It's just a monument.

33

And it's a shame. Because they're men. And it could have been their sons and their brothers. You know I stood there yesterday and watched a woman about fifty-five years old, she just sat down and cried, sat down on the pavement and cried, and I know her son was one of those names.

All we're doing here is glorifying war. That's all we're saying. They should have taken all the money, whatever it was that built this thing, and give it to the guys whose kids have defective hearts and defective throats, and are retarded because of something their daddies did. What about those kids? Who helps them? Who helps them? Who helps the guy who has been divorced three times? Look at this statue [laughs], is that supposed to relay the experience? Are you supposed to get your picture taken in front of it and say, "Hey, I've been to the Vietnam Veterans Memorial?" It's like the statue of Iwo Jima. And it's copyrighted. That's America.

The only reason I'm this way is because I'm just not gonna f—— quit, man. I'm not gonna let them beat me. If I survived that, I can survive anything.

If people knew what darkness was like! They think it gets dark over here. It never gets dark over here. We've got so many major cities, so many monuments, so many outside baseball games that the reflection is everywhere, that it never gets dark. Yeah, sure, it gets dark, but light reflects up, so even at night, light reflects up. Over there, there were no cities, no lights. When it got dark, it got dark. You couldn't see from here to there, pitch-black, ink-black! And they'd wait. In the monsoons it'd rain, in the dark. You'd be sitting there waiting for them, you couldn't fly, and they'd come through. . . .

You want to know how dark it is? Go home and sit in the darkest room and shut out all light, and think of the thing that terrifies you the most and think of it all night. That's what it's like for a whole year.

You know sometimes I get up at night and just turn the light on. I just turn on the light, stand in the middle of the bedroom and look around, and then turn off the light and go back to bed.

Terry and Priscilla Singleton of Baltimore visit their "name"—Edward Singleton, Jr., Terry's brother and the eldest of eight children. He was listed MIA in 1965 and later confirmed dead.

Justin Marble of Boston, a computer programmer. "The war is not something I really even heard much about . . . I'm twenty-four."

Anatol Konenenko of Philadelphia, POW-MIA activist. He is known as "Gimp" since both legs were paralyzed in Vietnam in 1969. "Willie Peter" is white phosphorous, the most dreaded antipersonnel weapon of the war. A single shell throws thousands of phosphorous particles; the burn cannot be extinguished.

Billy Odell of Corpus Christi is a crane operator on a Gulf Coast oil rig. He was a tunnel rat in Vietnam, 1966–68.

37

George Lopez is not a war veteran, but served in the USMC 1971–73. His brother was at Danang. He and his family visit the wall regularly.

Stanley Bey and Pamela El of Richmond, Virginia, have adopted an Islamic life. He was a weapons mechanic from 1971–72, serving in Thailand.

John Keefe and Paula S. Killion

John Keefe put on his fatigues again to come to the wall. It was like a pilgrimage for him; when he was not crying, he was talking.

Webster's got some incredible words for death—*kill, bought the farm*, and all, but the worst one is *wasted*. How many did you waste? . . . Look at them and what hurts is the waste. I helped a lot of guys come down but I don't have it myself. All around the mall you see life, birds . . . let the politicians argue. There'll always be two politicians who argue, but Vietnam needs to be remembered because there were fifty-eight thousand men and women who were alive—the cream of America—not because they were dead but because they were alive.

I cried when they died and I laughed when I survived. Today I decided I'll be proud I'm a Vietnam veteran—damn proud—they never ask why, they said go, and we went.

I never experienced more insanity in my entire life. Everything was going—machine-gun fire, artillery, air strikes—the first three days in country I was in my first firefight. I remember my M-16 in my hand, too scared to look out behind a wall, putting my gun over the top and just fast-firing—screaming at the top of my lungs, I don't know what I was screaming.

The world caved in on me two and a half years ago. What kicked me off was the dedication of this place. I watched with tears streaming down my face. I stared at the phone for six hours—I called up the Pawtucket, Rhode Island, outreach center. I have a love for food, and I had this image I couldn't get rid of. I loved baklava and my fear was that every layer I turned there would be another horror story. Then the stories started coming out. Why did they do it to me? It will never go away—and maybe I don't want it to go away—down on the wall I see my battery chief. I don't remember his name, but I can hear his words. I hear his voice and I don't even remember what he looks like and that hurts me.

Kenneth B. Goff: it's on this bracelet. Missing, sure. I went to high school with Kenny Goff, if you wanted the shirt off his back you wouldn't even have to ask. He once took his girlfriend out and my sister just to let my sister tag along. He didn't come back but he'll never be forgotten, not as long as I live and the English language. I hope the kids will remember, not that I won or lost, but that we weren't immoral—all these kids whose only thought was a six-pack of beer and a '59 Chevy and making time with the girl next door.

Two and half a years I was your stereotype. I was a drunk. I hung on to a job, God knows how. Remember, forty-eight hours after I got lifted out of the landing zone I was drinking beer in my father's yard—I wouldn't be surprised if the food I ate on the LZ [Landing Zone] was still in my system.

This year I went to my first Memorial Day parade, and I looked up in the clouds, and I saw those guys, and I said, "Welcome home." They asked me down to the American Legion for beer and sandwiches and I was torn between the emotion to hug the guy and say, "Where the f—— were you fifteen years ago?"

Gerald Fulkerson

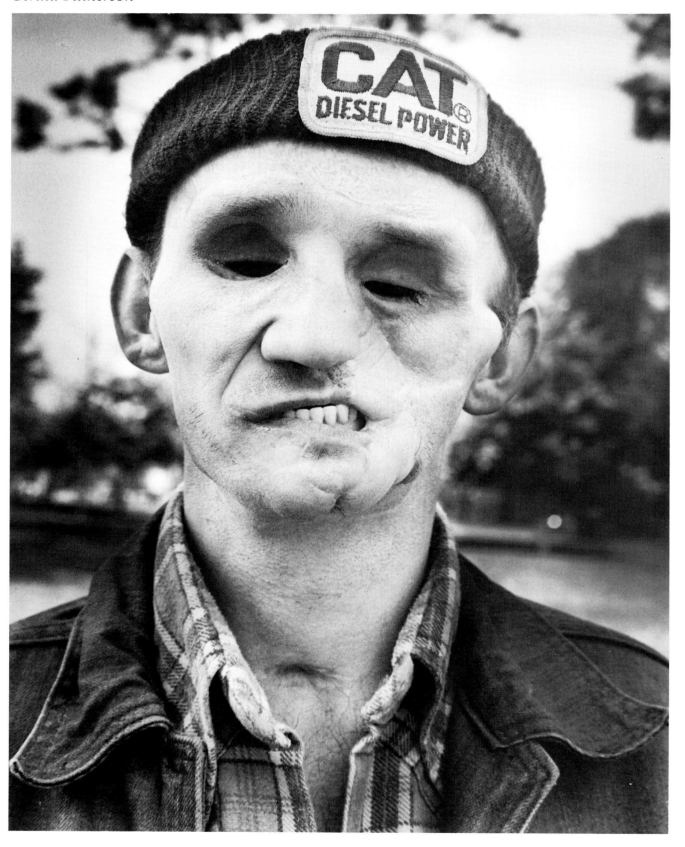

If you can't see, you wouldn't think you would get much out of it, but you get much more than you would know. I joined the Marine Corps right out of high school and I got through my year and the war without a scratch. You know how I got injured?—not Vietnam, hunting; the war didn't touch me.

I was preparing to go hunting, I was fooling around with my shotgun—winter in Michigan—there was a shell jammed in the barrel—I remember this all so clearly—and I was walking from my house to the garage when I slipped and that gun hit the floor and my chin hit the muzzle and from then on I was history. Maybe you'd like to know how blind people bowl. I'm a member of the Flint Blind Bowlers. You hang onto this rail that's about waist-high and it guides you and I think it's not much different from bowling with sight.

Now the blind bowlers are on tour and Washington was one of the stops and since I was in the military I wanted to see this. I had two Johns, John Novak and John Turner, friends of mine, a couple of months before we got home, they both got killed.

When I went to the wall I asked someone to put my hand on their names, I got a gut feeling—John and I were kind of close—when I put my hand there I said, "John, I am touching you again."

Lee Corn

Lee Corn is a sun-blasted carpenter from Stendahl, Indiana, with tiny scars all over his hands. He wanted a career in the military—he still wants a career in the military—but what he found there disillusioned him. He spent his year doing paperwork, sometimes near where battles raged; he felt his talents were wasted, and his work was wasted. Now, so long after the war, he's still working day to day.

I remember my return to the U.S. I remember I just wanted to come home and I just wanted to hear someone say we're proud of you. Now, you know, your family doesn't count in this. They are always going to say something like that. But it never happened. I remember one guy and I sitting in a bar just after I got back, and believe me there were spaces all around us in that bar because we were both in uniform. The bartender brought us a beer, and he says, "There's a businessman and he says, 'I don't care what everyone says, I think you guys did a hell of a job.'"

The other guy who was with me said, "What's this all about?" We didn't know it but that was the first and the last time for both of us.

Joe Bohannon and Carol Trent

Joe Bohannon is an unemployed landscaper, the recipient of shrapnel wounds and a bad conduct discharge. He volunteered in 1968.

I wanted to go to Vietnam and fight. Nobody in my family was ever in combat; the men all missed World War II, and my mother didn't want me to go, but my father said, "I'll sign the papers, I think every kid ought to go into the service."

Our outfit was called the Twenty-seventh Marines. It was made up of cooks, drivers. Everyone just gathered together, and one of the reasons there were so many people from Twenty-seventh Marines on the wall is they just threw us in together. We never even knew what a booby trap was: [General William] Westmoreland had asked for two hundred thousand more troops after Tet. That was us.

The first thing that we did was the guard duty on the road from Danang to Phu Bai—and unbelievably, a little kid that everyone had been tossing candy bars and K-rations to threw something back and it went off and badly wounded eight people. Everybody shot the kid. I thought, "What the hell! We're supposed to be helping these people?" I saw people take lighters to villages for no reason at all, just to do it. We would go out on nine-day patrol to do night ambushes in a platoon-sized unit and we would come back after three days and spend the rest of the time drinking beer.

I never understood why we were just hanging around like bait. Sometimes there were too many of them [the enemy] but the majority of the times there were only three to twelve people in an ambush—when there were too many, you just lay there and hope you didn't have the kind of guy in your platoon who's going to open up.

I enjoyed being out in the woods.

I got in enough trouble in the marines. I punched a captain and did four months in the brig for that, and that time doesn't count on your time in service. I did thirty days for not shaving, and another time I got forty-five days for borrowing an E2 uniform. When I got down to twenty-five days left they gave me guard duty but I refused to go out. I said it's time to go home: for that I got six months in the brig and a bad-conduct discharge.

I remember my mother up in the bedroom crying when I came home because of what I looked like. My uncle said I had changed, everyone said that. But my friends were the same, hanging out, playing pinball, they were just the same but their hair was long.

Most people were content to sit there and drink with you, and when they got drunk, they'd ask one question, "How many people did you kill?" They never really wanted to know what that world was like.

Saturday I went up to the book [listing the names on the memorial] and I found I couldn't remember their names. Sunday the names started coming back: ten or twelve boys I was around with, and Bobby, the only one who got killed, I sat here last night with a bunch of guys and more of the names started clicking back.

I came up here because I felt guilty. I felt I was the only Vietnam vet who hadn't been here, and the wall did take a lot of my guilt away. I felt I owed these guys a beer at least!

There's not that many people left alive from my outfit. Most of my team is dead—Allenbrook did them. I'm glad I was here and I think everyone should do that once, but I don't want to hear any more war stories, I know what they are, I want to know how these guys have adjusted to life now.

These people who are on the wall deserve to have us come here but we've been here for three days and I'm going to have nightmares for a week, and I don't deserve this, I'm not coming back. It's the world's largest headstone and what does it get you, your name on a piece of marble?

Jim and Brenda Smith with Jennifer, eleven, Jim, Jr., nine, Jan, six

I'm the superintendent of a roofing company. I was in Vietnam in '70. I was in the army artillery. I wasn't drafted, I enlisted. There are a couple of friends from Vietnam up here, and a couple of neighbors from Binghamton. They were killed in '68.

I used my veterans' benefits to go to vocational school. Getting into the army was just one of those things. I had lost my license, I didn't have no way to go of finding work in the area I was in, so I decided to take two years and go in the army and they sent me to Vietnam.

I thought it was nice that they finally did do something. I was in the Eight/Four Artillery, I can't even remember the division. I was the chief of section of the gun.

I would never want to go back over there, but I have good memories of the service.

49

Albert and Esther Shuler

We were a close-knit family, everything we did we did as a family—when my son was killed it just took something out of us. No one came forward. They never did tell us what happened. Nothing come out of it. We are as much in doubt today as we was the day they told us.

Our boy never did weigh over 150 pounds, and they sent us a body over 200 pounds.

If just one boy had come by who knew what happened to tell us what happened. All these years we've lived in doubt. It happened in 1969. He was twenty-one in December. He wrote me a letter and I told him, I said, "Now son, when you're twenty-one you'll be a man." So he wrote me a letter on his birthday. "Dad," he said, "I'm a man, I'm twenty-one." He spent that day in the jungle.

But there is something else. The government tells us that he was killed on the thirteenth. And there was four letters that he wrote on the fourteenth. From him, four people got four letters from him: his girlfriend, his nephew, and a little girl lives right below us that he went to church with. And you see, they never have explained that.

But his name is on the wall. I haven't got nothing against the military, having served in it. I've got nothing against the government. But looking at that wall I don't see how in the world a handful of barefooted peasants killed that many Americans.

Robert M. Staton, Jr., and family

My brother died in Vietnam. He was missing in action in '67. The wall has come to mean a great deal to Vietnam veterans, it's some kind of a reward for the job they did.

So I wanted to come to the wall for my mother—you know she still goes through a lot of changes. Because my brother, he never came home, his body didn't, we never did see it.

So I wanted to come by and rub the name. He was the older brother, born in '47. What he did, when he got out of high school—he was trying—you see I come from a family of ten—trying to go to school and my father couldn't afford to send him to school.

He got fed up one day and he volunteered for the military—airborne, he wanted to be a paratrooper. At the time he died he was with the 173d Airborne.

Honestly, the military sent us through so many changes you wouldn't believe it. It wasn't until 1968, they showed up one day, two people, my father wasn't home at the time. Two people they sent out to tell the family. I was the first person to see them and I went over to them and asked what they wanted.

They waited until he came home and told us what had happened. They said he was missing in action. And they wanted some pictures to see if they could identify some people in prison, so that if some writer or newsman could identify him, maybe he was captured.

We had already been told that his body was on a ship, and the body was supposed to come back to Rocky Mount, North Carolina. We were willing to accept the fact that he had died over there and his body was on the way home. We had already hired an undertaker and called the funeral home.

Then we waited. 'Cause when the body gets there, they are supposed to call the undertaker to go pick it up. But they never called the undertaker. He never got a call at all. It went on for a couple of months. We kept expecting it.

We had to call Fort Bragg. We had to call *them* up.

I went in behind him and the brother behind me went in and my niece went in, all of us went into the army. I had orders for Vietnam, but I knew I could get out of it because of my brother and I had never told them. The army didn't care.

We didn't know much about Vietnam. The only thing we knew was from the TV. They were in so much pain. My parents didn't like the fact that they were fighting. They always asked the question, "Why are they fighting?" We didn't seem like we accomplished anything, and it seems like he died in vain.

After we had called, they came back, you know, and they finally admitted that they didn't know where he was—that took three months. And then they wanted to send us a casket with bricks in it, but my sister, who was the oldest at the time, said no. She made this decision. She'd rather have nothing. We had a memorial service.

Magnolia, Amos, and Mae Williams

Very southern, gentle, and respectful of Washington, the Williams family drove from Webster, Florida, to Washington on the way to take the Williams grandson, the huge-framed Albert Eddie, to his first-year's orientation week at East Tennessee State. The family's patriarch, S. Sgt. Eddie Lee Williams was declared dead in 1975, nine years after he disappeared on a combat mission. The grandson still wears his POW/MIA bracelet. Amos Williams is Sergeant Williams's brother; Magnolia Williams, his mother.

AMOS WILLIAMS: I think it's good. I like it because you can look here and you can find all the names. Eddie Lee was a sergeant-major, he was in service twenty-five years. They sent him out on some secret combat mission and he never returned. We traveled all the way to see my brother's name up here. I had never been in Washington. It will give the family something to remember.

MAGNOLIA WILLIAMS: It makes me feel relieved. It takes the anxiety out of my heart that he's up there after all these years. This is really beautiful.

Mimo Robinson and family

Mimo Robinson is married to the headmaster of a small New England prep school and has that certain stance, accent, and look of the upper crust. Hers was the class that avoided the war while poor boys fought. One exception was her first husband, who from a background similar to hers, moved against the tide.

My first husband was Bruce B. Warner; we were married in 1964 and he died in '66. He was a graduate of Hotchkiss, Yale class of '64 and a member of Wolf's Head.

Bruce felt that going into the Marine Corps was a kind of a passage. He did Naval Reserve Officers Training at Yale and then they sent him to Quantico.

He was sent out to Okinawa in February of 1965—he was there for a year—and in February of 1966 we got word that he had been wounded. A sergeant came at three A.M. and said that he'd been wounded, but not to worry, because if it were bad he'd have sent for the next of kin. We had only been married six months, it didn't occur to me that I was next of kin.

We got a flight over immediately in a plane—with all these kids who were *going* to Vietnam. They were all on their way to this thing with their pictures of their girlfriends; and the planes for military transport are not like the usual planes—they are simply bare.

Bruce had been on a volunteer scouting mission and he had been shot five times. He was really bad. He was lucid only some of the time. He was in traction, his abdomen had been opened, he was in constant pain. He was at Clark Field in the Philippines for ten days and he had improved. We looked at Bruce as pretty good compared with what he had been.

After ten days the doctors said he should go home because of the danger of disease in that hospital. I think what finally killed him was the traveling. The pressure in the airplanes was awful. He was cut everywhere, from top to bottom.

In the end when we got back to San Francisco, a friend from Yale, Jay Huffert, came to see Bruce. There were three layovers as we flew across the country. And then there was a terrible ride to St. Alban's Hospital in Long Island. We had to scream at the driver to slow down. Bruce was in terrible pain.

He lived for a week and a half. He had lost one kidney and the other failed. He talked quite a bit; he just wanted to go back to Hotchkiss and teach there, where he was in prep school. In the end it was heart failure.

In the beginning of the war I was glad Bruce wanted to go. He was very patriotic. But now, looking at that monument, it is the first one that calls war the way it is.

Gene Isaacs

Gene Isaacs is a man of the "jus' a good ol' boy" variety who made a good thing out of the Vietnam Memorial. By day, and more particularly on weekends, his Dodge van sat on the east side of Twentieth Street, across Constitution Avenue from the screen of trees, the artificial lake, the tall elms and landscaping that keep the monument invisible. There with the tray of T-shirts and the stuffed cartons poking out from the inside of the van, a large Doberman Pinscher wore a cross with a chrome-plated chain.

Gooks are not gooks even though they all look the same. For instance the guy next to us with the stand used to be a major in the Vietnamese air force. We've been staying at Bull Run Regional Park and coming here in the daytime, we kind of like it out there and we hope to stay in Washington until Veteran's Day. We're hoping there's some money in it—the T-shirts, and I'll tell you women will buy them for their husband when the husband wouldn't buy it themselves. I've got four kids and I'm trying to get a disability from the government, I've got Agent Orange real bad on my legs and my arms.

Do you know they've got a big warehouse full of the stuff people have left at the wall, and that there's been a dozen guys guns to their heads at night, and the vets talked them out of it? And the wall weeps. Water comes down on the letters and they disappear and there are those who say that the water comes right out of the names.

George Ash is a member of a motorcycle club for Vietnam vets only. A former light weapons specialist, he is still in the army.

George Big, a Navajo, served with Special Forces in Vietnam, the last assignment of his career as a professional soldier.

60

Charles J. Blais, itinerant carpenter, was an enlisted man with the 173d Airborne Brigade in 1967–68.

Leverett Preble, law librarian of the Library of Congress. He was a combat engineer officer, 1967–68.

Gregory David Douglas

A combat infantryman with the Seventh and later the Eighth Armored Cavalry Division, Gregory Douglas volunteered in the summer of 1970, four days before Independence Day.

Many times decorated, a Bronze Star winner, he became "Brother D.C." to his unit. He was wounded several times, the worst being a mine blast that damaged his entire left side and resulted in second- and third-degree burns over large areas. On his return home, he was to find that his mother, a semiliterate woman, had not been receiving his pay as he had instructed while in country; neither had he. Douglas claims many things, and among them that the government has never paid him for his tour. He is unemployed.

Y asee, North Vietnam could come down and dictate to the South Vietnam because they was scared as heck of the North Vietnam because the North Vietnam was trained the same way we were—guerrilla—so the South Vietnam wasn't that much of a threat to us 'cause they really had a heart, but like part of their living conditions were terrible. See, they comes out of the trees, they come out of the ground, they come out of bunkers, and—they was experts. The average G.I. expended a lot of waste ammunition. We also had these heavy rucksacks on our backs, we also had to lug a whole case of Coke—that was part of our rations, Coca-Cola—you'd pay for it out of your money, so a whole case of Coca-Cola—I carried a whole case of Coca-Cola for forty-five days over in Vietnam. You didn't have no hotplates or anything, you ate out of cans.

See, that's your conditions. Now a lot of people think the men had it easy. Man, I didn't have no bath, I didn't take any showers, you slept in your clothes, you did everything in your clothes. I caught a rash my first week over there and my sergeant, he said to me, "Brother D.C.," I said, "What's up, Sar?" (Because they don't call you by your name, they call you by your state, so if you see someone from your state they'll bring him to you and they'll say, "Hey man, here's your home." So that's letting you know that you have a person from your home, so they call him "home," or "Hi, what's happening back in the world," referring back to your state.) But getting back to your living conditions and food conditions in Vietnam, I like to pause and say that, before I continue on with this nonsense.

I stayed from September, I stayed for three months in the hospital. I got blowed up in an explosion. C-4. I caught on fire. My whole body was a Roman candle, meaning the only thing that saved my life was by me stepping on the explosion, it lifted me up and raised me from that which would have swept me there.

The thing about Vietnam, nope, it's not the point of you getting quick. Vietnam, from the experienced person in the field, Vietnam will teach you two things, that's patience and discipline. . . . If you want to come back, you want to have plenty of patience, and you must be well disciplined.

What I'm saying, is that being in Vietnam, my arrival time as referring back to Agent Orange, as most people say, post-traumatic stress, whatever term they're going to use, is that as far as Agent Orange is concerned, I feel as though women, volunteers, and any individual who represented the United States of America should be entitled to any types of money that he or she is entitled to. The reason I'm saying that is that they used items such as food when they were using the chemicals, I can't say right off what year they started using it. What I'm leading up to is that you were exposed to the chemical through these means of survival, meaning milk, water, and the water you used to dilute it, because I mean the milk over there was so daggone thick that if you used the original milk, it was real thick, white milk as well as chocolate. So the chemicals they sprayed was in the water. Secondly, the food, you had to eat, and thirdly the clothes. And you're also breathing the air.

That was the worst thing in the world they could do—Agent Orange. The purpose was to kill off the foliation. In three days to a week, all the vegetation would die. But now, that left you without shelter. Being a combat infantryman, confinement was a must. You dealt with three, maybe four types of terrain. You can't compare Vietnam with any other war; because of the terrain you got the single, double, and triple canopy, and when I say canopy, we're talking about jungle. It's hard to travel, and you've got a heavy rucksack on your back, and the enemy they didn't have that, they're traveling light. The only time you might see them heavy down is that they might be carrying supplies, money, or rice. They can live off the land. They was very light, a run and a shovel. By the time they got to us, we was very exhausted. I'd go sometimes three days without food and water and some days two nights without rest—that's the way you've been trained. The professional infantryman can go that long.

People say the Vietnam veteran's nothing but alcoholics and druggies. I think that's a very stereotype thing. There's quite a few veterans exposed to alcohol and drugs. That's all races. For instance, I'm out of the military and I'm having these problems. I come to you and tell you I'm having these problems. They tell you, well, you're crazy, you're on drugs, you're on alcohol. That's not normal. But when you're in the military it's an everyday thing, okay? For instance, one is accepted and one is not accepted. So basically it's messed up.

Getting back to these clothes and sex—a lot of guys are having these babies with Vietnamese women and any kind of women, it doesn't matter, I mean love is love and it comes in all colors. A lot of guys—I've experienced going to these meetings, these programs on Vietnam veterans for a very long time, and one thing I would say is that the women have not paid their dues, they have not served in the field, so therefore they shouldn't be entitled to anything. But they have post-traumatic stress, the volunteers and the nurses. Any individual who was over there, that ate the food, drank the milk, breathed the air, and wore the clothes, he or she was exposed [to Agent Orange]. They should get equal treatment because they were there. I've been to the VA hospital for the past ten years. I get sixty percent disability, and that helps support me; I'm still living with my family. What a lot of people fail to realize is that once you're a Vietnam veteran you can apply for a job, and I've been sure they needed help, and when you check "veteran," you are considered, you are never employed.

My experience when I came home, was my parents asked me where was the money. I never received any money—the military never sent any of the money home. I had applied for it. There wasn't any welcome mat throwed out for me when I got in. My mother was more glad to see me, and then to be concerned about the money. Most of my friends that served in Vietnam got killed. Like I was saying, I was checking on the wall for the ones who got killed.

So you notice, I don't show no emotions. I was trying to calm a white gentleman down because he had lost his composure because he had lost his son, see, he's dealing from the heart, and when you dealing from the heart, you show emotion. See, when you deal from the brain, you don't show emotions, and that's why I had a lot of problem relating with my family, my friends and all, because I don't show emotion. When my nephew got killed, my sister got angry at me 'cause I didn't show emotions. I didn't cry. I showed my concern. I was the only one that maintained my composure. When my mother died, my sisters and brothers got angry because I didn't show emotions and they were in tears. I don't want you to get the impression that if you don't—like people say, if you don't look a person in the eye that's a weakness—that's a lie. Because a lot of people can't look people in the eye. I'm saying not the point of being strong or anything, that's just the way I have been conditioned. I know the war is over, but I still live with this hell, meaning I have excessive sweating, from the malaria, it comes in spurts.

People gave me a hard time for being a veteran, meaning, personally, I'm not speaking of other veterans. When I come out, I went to several counselors to try to get in the work force—and afterwards I couldn't get a job, so I went back to school in art and data processing, and I'm saying people didn't really help or not help. Vietnam was an unpopular war and they kept a lot from veterans. And from being a black individual, blacks was denied a lot of privileges. From my experience and my reading, the only thing veterans want is what's due me. You're talking about giving veterans all this money—it's so daggone late. So late, and now they're giving them all these ceremonies, and why so late, and you talk about a lot of guys who are really bent out of shape. I might use some slang referring to the hostage situation. That's the biggest problem, these guys receive a Purple Heart, receive all this news.

Equal justice under law. See, I found a lot of white guys as well as foreigners, too. That white-and-black thing, man, is out. Used to talk about a lot of hate—racist groups and all that. The hate groups that's out there, they're scared—in the sense that the individual's a threat. The general public doesn't know what the individual's going to do. They think that because a person's on drugs and alcohol he can do anything—they think all of them's alcohols and druggies. But that one individual, he can kill up a lot of individuals. Incidentally, there was a guy out here that killed *him*self.

You see a lot of people got killed in Vietnam. While you're sitting here in D.C. or whatever state, chilling out, meaning relaxation, it was killing people. When people was coming home, two days out of Vietnam, like one guy, he was white, and his father embraced him, he was probably glad to see him come home, and his dad said, "Well, I know everything is all right now and I know they're in Saigon and they're doing well. . . ." and the guy said, "Dad, how is it that the media could lie to you so much due to the fact that the war is unpopular?" They were still killing people over there. That was no holiday. All right.

I'd like to accomplish a lot of things. I've never been married. I've never had any children. I would like to get married and have some children one day. But I feel like the public. . . .

I would kill men, women, children while I was there, anything and everything. See, that's what they trained me for. The seek, find, and destroy have two meanings. So we went with the second. The Vietnamese people must take into consideration some factors. The American is not used to that terrain, number one, he had a heavy load. He got dehydrated, he caught malaria, plus he had all this heavy stuff on. The Vietnamese didn't wear all that—they were in their home. The guys in the other wars didn't have to deal with tunnels.

One Veterans Administration doctor tells me it's a miracle I'm alive. I was medevacked from the field three or four times, and would be given three days to a week to recover. But the V.C. often fought in the field bearing serious wounds. Men in my unit had a good deal of respect for the V.C., calling them Sir Charles, or sometimes, not as often as is thought, "Mister Charlie," but not meaning it in the derogatory sense of "Charlie," the white boss.

Service made me mature. In the field, we were treated worse than animals. It really would give you the blues. And then we'd have to go back and fight. Some guys would count how many they killed, but I didn't . . . I could be cold about killing, but I didn't have an ego thing about it. You lived with your head, which can be cold and calculated, and didn't live within your heart, which shows too much emotion.

That one [motioning to the Three Soldiers statue] I like better; this I think is very cold. I guess that's the impression they're trying to give, but it's just lifeless and black and cold. It's very creepy. And the reflection you see of yourself in the wall makes it so . . . scary. And the similarities between Nicaragua and Vietnam. I really would not like to see another monument like this over there.

I think it's interesting how they say at the top, "These are the people who died in honor of the Vietnam War"—that they would say "Vietnam War"! I thought they would say "service in Vietnam," because it wasn't a war. I was surprised that they said that.

If you look in the eyes of the guys in the statue, especially the one furthest to the right, I don't know how he did it, but you look at him and you know he just does not want to be there and you don't get any feelings like this from these walls. Each one of these names has a whole story behind it, like those three people, but you just don't get that feeling from these walls. Name after name after name, until they just become letters pushed together; they're not people any more.

67

Colonel Murray (left) *and Jerry Rogers Todd*

There have been marriages at the wall, but no funerals. And there have been many reenlistments. This was an important moment for Jerry Todd, a career air force analyst, and his colonel. Both are veterans of the war.

MURRAY: I'd like to say that for me, it is an honor for you to select me to reenlist you at this time. So let's go on with that right now. Raise your right hand, please. Repeat after me: I (and state your full first name) . . .

TODD: I, Jerry Rogers Todd.

MURRAY: Do solemnly swear and affirm that I will support and defend the Constitution of the United States—against all enemies, foreign and domestic—that I will bear true faith and allegiance—to the same—that I will obey the orders of the president—and the orders of the officers appointed over me—according to regulations and the uniform Code of Military Justice—so help me God.

TODD: [*Repeats*]

MURRAY: We got you again!

Phyllis Fisher

Five of my boys are on the wall. Three of the five were my students. Stanley Bradley was my student in 1956 in Georgia when I was teaching the seventh grade there. His feet wouldn't even touch the floor. He was a very Christian little boy who always helped his friends, especially with the math, because he was good. He had written an article for some national magazine and it was published the weekend of his death.

The father was a judge, and he was sitting on the bench, and the moment the officers walked in he said he knew why they were there. And he wrote Mr. Nixon and said, "Why? Why my son?"

I moved to Cherryville, North Carolina, to teach, and one of my first students was Bobby Anthony, and of course Bobby had a great deal of difficulty with work, but he was very patient, and tried so hard to learn. Bobby's father was a World War II veteran. Bobby was not killed by an enemy bullet, but he was killed by our own men. He was in a rice paddy, and a patrol boat in the river ordered them to identify themselves and hardly gave them a chance to do it, and fired on them and killed twenty-two of them, and Bobby was one.

Larry Sane was another student from Cherryville—an eighth-grader. A very happy-go-lucky, warm, friendly child who cared about others, and his caring was the thing that led to his death because he was on a patrol with his unit and they ran into an ambush, and of course, Larry with the nature that he was, he stuck out his arms—he had on a poncho and he stuck out him arms and veered off to the side and drew the enemy fire off to him, waving his arms, and saved the other guys. He left a little girl and his wife.

Tom Shepard, I did not teach, but he was in school and I knew him. He died February 22, 1967.

Keith Heavner, I did not teach, but I taught his sister. He was on duty at an outpost and it was time for his R & R, but he wanted to go on R & R with his buddies in two weeks, and in the course of the two weeks, they were ambushed and he was killed.

It was a small town, 5,280 people, and we lost four people, and a neighboring town, even smaller, lost nine.

My husband was a World War II veteran, got shot all to pieces in Leyte [Gulf]. My own boy, all those years I was thinking that he would have to go to Vietnam. But when they pulled the numbers, it was on his birthday, he got the number 250, too high for the draft, and to this day the number 250 is on his door inside his bedroom.

71

James Ryan

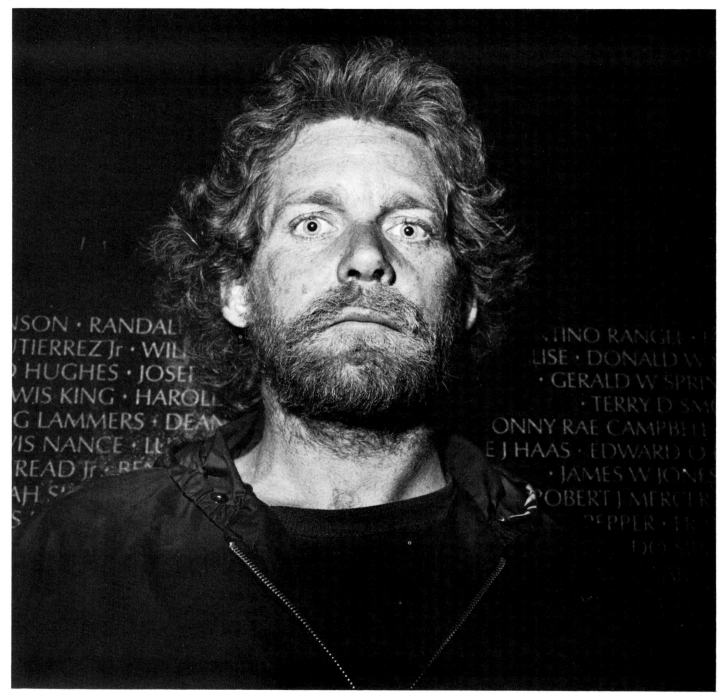

James Ryan was a night visitor who stopped on his way through the capitol. Unaffected by the war himself, he knew veterans and felt drawn to the wall to find his cousin's name. He is a truck driver from New York City.

The man I think about is my cousin, who was twenty years old when he was killed in 1968, but he couldn't even get a beer.

He was in the Tet offensive and got shot in the face three times. My uncle had to identify him by the spider tatoo on his arm. And the f—— War Department got the name spelled wrong (it's spelled Pyakptak) so they spent a day running around thinking it was a mistake. They had to go to the funeral home and look at the spider.

Sergeant Major John "Top" Holland

Top Holland's face shines like some dull pile of coals, with the bulges and lumps of twenty-six years of soldiering, and his body beneath it is all that could be expected from that kind of life, a barrel set on two stout legs, with shoulders set habitually straight. He is one of many "hard case" sergeants inevitably called "Top."

But Holland's days of fighting are over now, and his uniform jacket, the one with so much campaign ribbon on the left breast that it looks like a shield of many colors, is something he wears fondly, and strokes like an old man, and folds carefully. He is a property manager in Alexandria, Virginia, and he has fought in every United States war from World War II to Vietnam. He is at the memorial for several weeks helping younger men gather petitions to ask some international body to investigate the possibility (to men like him a certainty) that there are missing men in Vietnam.

When I heard about Grenada, I said, "Goddam, they gave a war and didn't even invite me" . . . but my son Eric was in Lebanon at least.

I was twenty-six years in, twenty-six and out, and I had to go back and teach ROTC. It was twenty-three years in the army and four in the Marine Corps. From day to day it changes down here. Some days it's nothing but families, and then there are some days when you don't sell one shirt. When I first saw it, I wasn't too impressed with it, but goddam, it grows on you. The first time I went down there by myself, it was dark and drizzling, and the damn place seemed to close in around you. . . . The petition will be delivered to the Vietnamese delegation at the U.N. asking them to give an accounting of the 2,480 Americans who are still unaccounted for in Vietnam.

On many days, hundreds of objects are left at the wall—they are flow-ers and flags, medals, letters, photos, and a bewildering variety of other things, from marijuana cigarettes to beer cans to stuffed toys. The offerings are unique to the Vietnam Veterans Memorial; the effect is semireligious, almost surely pagan—offerings to the dead.

The more durable of these objects, since November 1984, have been gathered and stored, sorted and catalogued, and eventually placed in cabi-nets in a temperature- and humidity-controlled warehouse at Glenn Dale, Maryland, with the improbable acronym of MARS, for Museum and Arche-ological Regional Storage Facility. There, beside second-rank portraits of Lincoln and furniture from historic houses under United States Park Ser-vice jurisdiction, lie the things from the wall. No one ever expected that the wall would become a magnet for these offerings, which range from battle medals to ragged clothing—and no one knew exactly what to do with them. But they kept coming, in spite of the fact that they are gathered in by Park Service rangers every day.

Under the law, objects left at the memorial become abandoned after thirty days and United States property. No decision has been made on the future of the wall collection, but MARS curators regard it as uniquely val-uable, a record of silent acts that show how people felt in the aftermath of the war.

Donald L. Sargent's hat

Yeah. It was eighteen years. It was August 1968 and the story behind [it] is that I was with the One/Nine Cavalry and I was a machine gunner in a helicopter—I was twenty-one or twenty-two at the time, a seventh-grade dropout, and at that particular time I could hardly read and write. I met this guy Littlejohn.

He was a Berkeley graduate. He was a very intelligent young guy. He kept trying to get me to finish high school. For about six months we flew together. Actually, we hated each other a great deal—as a matter of fact, one day I almost shot him. We flew sister ships.

And one morning his ship went out early on what they call a "sniffer" mission, and all of a sudden we got a radio signal back from one of the tank commanders that a helicopter had gone down, and he verified that it was Littlejohn's ship. A warrant officer on my ship told me that he didn't think there was anyone alive on that ship.

I remember the jeep coming down, the Red Cross jeep with the medics, and they threw two plastic bags on the ground next to us. I got very angry about that—to them it was an everyday occurrence, it didn't mean much. We put the bags on the ship and we flew out, and as we were coming in for a landing—it was a hot landing zone. And I waited as we landed and all of a sudden I saw the two bags in the back of the ship, two of them right next to where I was sitting, they literally just threw them under the gun into the ship, and I could see Littlejohn's arm. The strangest thing that happened, I guess when I looked at him—I knew it was him—I said, "Better you than me, Littlejohn."

And then I became angry with myself and felt more pity and sorrow. It was like he was still alive though he was dead. I mean I could still feel him. I said that after that, I would live a life for two.

I was shot down two weeks after that, but I still kept flying after that—and to make a long story short, I flew back to the States, came into San Francisco, I think it was, wintertime. They treated us like dirt at the terminal. Gave us a clean set of uniforms and sent us home. It had only been twenty-four hours from a combat mission; it was like being thrown from night to day—into a society that . . . I didn't even know how the hell I was supposed to act!

I went back to Boston, came into the airport, and there was nobody there to visit me. Nobody knew I was home. It was snowing and I was in a short-sleeved shirt. Well, after Boston I went back to Virginia to Fort Eustis. After the army had spent all that money to send me into aviation, and they sent me back to Fort Eustis as a tank mechanic.

I met a girl there. I met her on a Monday night, we had three dates, and we were married that following Sunday. I was shipped to Germany, thinking about Littlejohn (who will be with me for the rest of my life). I started my high school diploma. I went at nighttime. It took me two years to finish it. I went back to the States; I went after my bachelor's in art, finished my bachelors, then I went after my master's in art, and I finished my master's.

Then I taught for five years at a private high school, the Orme School in Arizona. I was an art teacher, and I also taught humanities and was survival instructor (because of Vietnam I knew quite a bit about survival). I taught young kids. I became very friendly with all these young people; I was always talking about Vietnam and trying to emphasize humanities as much as possible to the fourteen- to twenty-two-year-olds, to try to give them an idea of what it meant to be in a war, from the flag-waving, God-bless-America aspects to the inhumanity of the Vietnam War, not just on the Vietnamese people, but on the American people also.

That lasted until my wife and I divorced; I had a little boy, eight, the little boy and I stayed in Arizona two more years trying to survive as an artist. I joined the National Guard. It was like going back to mother. Now I'm a therapist and illustrator at Fort Eustis, and I'm working on my master's thesis.

Littlejohn was killed in '68. You know Littlejohn was not really his name, I never knew his name.

I stole that medal from Littlejohn in 1968 two days before he was killed, and I held it for eighteen years, and then I brought it back hoping that by doing so I'd cut some ropes to my past. The other medals you see there are mine because . . . I was shot down . . . I felt that I should have been on the wall.

I stole that medal because I hated him. He was a graduate student, he was drafted, and he hated Vietnam; and I wanted an Air Medal so bad. I took it—borrowed it—for eighteen years. By borrowing his medal it was like having him with me.

Bill Robinson

Bill Robinson is unemployed and had just enough money to make the trip with a group of his fellow Florida vets. A pilgrimage to the wall. His friends say he's still seriously affected by the war, and indeed he proudly wears the mysterious dark card on his hat. He is fond of saying that a United States card company sent thousands of packs of cards to Vietnam—with fifty-two aces of spades in each pack.

To wear the ace of spades on your hat meant something. In the Buddhist religion, if you left that sign on a body, they wouldn't touch it—it was a fearful symbol to the mind of some Orientals, a body would simply stay where it was until it rotted into the jungle.

John Paine

I am the founder and president of the Gay Veterans Association—national. I enlisted in the army out of high school in New York, and I would have made a career out of it. I joined because it was an obligation, I felt.

But when my homosexuality was disclosed I was forced out—a general discharge under honorable conditions—perhaps that was why I decided to do something about it. Homosexuality runs rampant in the military, and it's not just the privates and the sergeants but the majors, the colonels, even the generals.

The thing is that as long as it's kept below ground it's tolerated, but as soon as something gets down on paper, you get pushed out. A despondent lover turned me in.

Some of us are Vietnam veterans, some of us are World War II veterans. The United States doesn't want a gay person defending the country. In fact, they don't want a gay person at all! After a year and a half, the GVA has got six hundred people as members; I was able to participate in a wreath-laying ceremony at Arlington on Memorial Day at the Tomb of the Unknown Soldier. Think of it. There could be a gay in there!

It's not right to say if a person is gay he can't serve. I've always thought that every individual who graduates from high school should serve in the military. When a person has been in the Vietnam War all alone, who is he going to turn to to release his sexual tension if not his fellow soldier?

The American government puts up these monuments for people and then forgets about them, instead of doing things for the people that are still alive. The government should get rid of the homophobic atmosphere within the military. We're not just doctors and lawyers, we're in the military, too, and bullets don't choose.

James Lewis and family

The Lewises are a nice, straight American family from Columbia, South Carolina, where Jim works as senior structural engineer for a large engineering firm. He is a veteran of the war, an air force military policeman who volunteered in 1966 and served his year in country from July 1968 to 1969. The Lewises are looking for a name on the wall, the name of a friend, a West Pointer who was shot down and killed.

I served in Vietnam myself and this is one thing I wanted to see while I was here. It seems all the names strike you as the fact that human life was sacrificed, just like I saw when I served—but the nation didn't support it. It makes you think, why did all these men die, and literally in vain? I've seen them crying here, and I know sometimes a good cry helps clear things up.

Adolfo Lugo

Adolfo Lugo loomed out of the darkness at midnight, walking from a moving van he was driving south from New York. He was a truck driver, yes, but he said he had another career as well, managing talent, actors and models. He went into the army at nineteen and is glad he did.

I just came from the New York veterans' march, and what it says to me is they're trying to tell us: "You did a good job—you get a little parade—now go home."

I spent my time as a cop in Saigon—an MP. In the army, they tell you don't get too close to any one guy, and I had one guy, a friend, seventeen years old, he got killed because he did point while I was doing slack. I told the captain, "Either get me out of the field or I'm going to kill someone." He was a West Point guy, the kind that says, "Go get some medals and get shot," but I got the transfer.

Saigon at the end of 1969, for me it was good—there was not that much action—of course, the AWOLs were always trying to kill MPs; one night some of us walked into a bar and one lieutenant killed two MPs. But we got hot water and we got a lot of food and I stuck it out for fourteen months.

When I got home, people treated me good—free drinks, free food. I wore my uniform. You got to remember, some of these veterans, they exaggerate. I kept myself busy—I found a girl who kept me busy. When I thought about Vietnam I'd go crazy, do things like wreck records and my stereo, and one time I had a nightmare, woke up, grabbed her and almost choked her.

A lot of these guys are seeking something for themselves. They want the government to do everything. A lot of these guys are waiting for someone else to do something. I'm not like some of these guys who are hurting who got drafted. The army got me out of the slums, it got me a house and two years of college.

I got something. Maybe it's true, there is a type of guy who likes danger and wants to see what it's all about. But some of the officers, they were just like *Apocalypse Now*, they want to get a high body count for the captain. I had to kill little kids and all that.

The officers only served four months. I think, let them all serve twelve months. And about the antiwar, I felt that if those people had left us alone and let the generals play their war games, I would have got home a lot earlier. But let's say I'm glad I'm not up there.

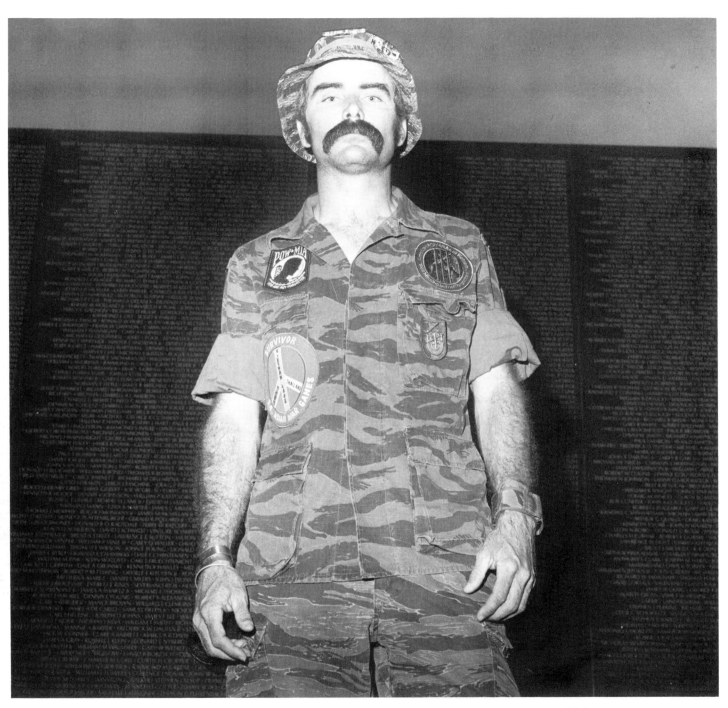

Bill Callahan had already completed the Florida-Washington portion of his East Coast hike for POW/MIA causes when he visited the memorial. He has only one leg, and was later hit by an apparently malicious driver while on the way to New York to join in the May 1985 veterans' celebration. His injuries were not serious.

Jeffrey Budzis

Jeffrey Budzis waited until he drank his quart bottles of beer in paper sacks before walking up to the memorial. Most of the day and into dusk he sat in the grove like a trooper, in the shadows looking out, waiting. He talked, incessantly, intelligently, to anyone who would listen throughout the day, until the listeners would drift away as if burned by his intensity.

I have been asking myself why I am here for the past two days. I was sure that if I didn't come this time I wouldn't come. This is the closest to the wall I have ever been and why this is I don't know.

I was there from 1967 to 1968 with the Fifth Marine Regiment. I was a grenadier, just a grunt. The reason was I dropped out of high school in '67 and I joined. It was *The Sands of Iwo Jima*, the John Wayne movies, "go be a hero," all twisted together—but everything works out in the end. I had screwed off in high school. I guess you could say I came from a typical low-income family.

In the Marine Corps, in the very first hour, they break that attitude. I was very proud to be in the Marine Corps and I still am. In those years it was just assumed and expected that if you were in the USMC that you would go to Vietnam. I felt good about it. I felt pride. I had a good sense of accomplishment. And even in my tour in Vietnam it wasn't too bad. I only got wounded once and that was minor.

If there is a message to my attitude, it's not to forget; because I don't think history will ever record what went on there. You would be sitting there and all of a sudden a new officer would walk by. And most of the guys who died over there died in the first two weeks of their time and the last two weeks. In my tour I did a lot of combat, I did a lot of jungle, and recently I even found myself in a history book about the Vietnam War.

The trouble is I don't remember anything happening the way it was written in that book. The way I remember in this particular action we got our asses kicked and the book made it like we had held the enemy off. What I remember was they came right through us and down the other side.

When I got back, people wouldn't know you. Now all this is going on. For ten years and stuff. For me, it's eighteen years, and now it's the Vietnam veteran who is better than anyone else. Well, I didn't smoke and I didn't drink booze and fifteen minutes outside of the wire you were in the boondocks.

For a long time after I got back I wondered whether I had changed or what. It was so hard to distinguish honesty. It was hard to get people to talk about Vietnam, but there certainly was a need to. All people wanted was some kind of Hollywood version. I guess you could say I didn't do real well adjusting. I spent my time bumming around, I went back to school, and I quit. Between 1969 and 1973 I was here and there, helter-skelter all over the country. I had one wife, I had two wives, and neither one seemed to have a sense of humor. There was no place to go but I could still move.

For all of us, the terror, the horror, of Vietnam—whatever you want to call it—that thing in Vietnam. It was so real, so alive, that when you hit the U.S., there was this emotional boredom. You would see some guy in a car tearing up the street and you'd say to yourself, "Why—wow, what a stupid move!" Vietnam influenced getting close to people—you didn't really want to.

I am sitting here today and I still feel the same way. I got 50 percent disability for delayed stress, and that's a hard thing for a marine. I thought of staying in when I got back, but by then it seemed that even the Marine Corps had turned against you, that you were used merchandise, that they had got what they wanted and now you were just extra. So I spent three months at Camp Pendleton. I wasn't sleeping good and a corpsman who bunked near me says, "You go see the doctor, get a checkup."

I went to see the doctor and the next thing I know I'm sent up with the Military Police and they put me in a closed ward, and all I had been doing was checking my weapon and cleaning it every day. When they found I wasn't going to hurt anyone they kind of let me alone.

When I killed somebody over there it wasn't a good feeling and it wasn't a bad feeling—I didn't laugh and I didn't throw up. It's the same at this memorial. I stayed up all last night listening to this camaraderie stuff. Brother, you went to Vietnam alone and I felt like going to the memorial alone. The reason I put on my fatigues was that I knew after all this publicity I'd have no trouble, even looking funny, but yesterday I did feel weird—I got out of a cab and people were asking me to let them take a picture of me with their kid.

I can't handle people thanking me. What are they thanking me for?! I think I understand what people are trying to do, it's just too late.

Ever since Vietnam I have become a night person. I guess I feel that somebody's got to be on watch. And I don't want to forget, you can't forget, and I am actually afraid when people tell me, "Why don't you forget?" because you can't forget any of history, it breaks the stream.

I don't want people to forget but I find it very hard to remember myself. If I were to put my whole Vietnam memory on a film, it wouldn't make three hours.

When I first heard about the wall, I didn't like it. I didn't like organization. Last July I busted into a parade. I wanted to get in it but I didn't want to go through channels. I just showed up on the parade grounds. Naturally, it was a Fourth of July parade, and there was no part in it for Vietnam veterans. Last Friday in Green Bay I sold $144 worth of poppies in front of a store. I thought of bringing some stuff here to the memorial and leaving it, but what could I leave? The only thing was a picture of me taken in Danang, but when I looked at it, it was as if it was not me but my kid or something and I guess it would be my kid now. Anyway, I don't think I understand the memorial, which is why I can't go near it. If you had fifty thousand pennies stacked up I could understand it, but these are people, and nobody can think of a reason yet. It seems to me sometimes that every one of these people's families should get one share of Dow Jones stock from the government—that would make it clear.

Coming here was the most difficult thing I have done in years—maybe I'll become a senator, maybe that's it! But the trouble is I don't want to make any commitments. And our country didn't want to make any commitments, it broke its commitments, but since the government is an enigma, no one got blamed.

The gestures that we make are too late. We say, "Okay, here's your reward," and we say, "Now stop and go away—okay, take the three statues, any number of statues, just go away." I have my own demands. I want five acres of land and I want the government to open the book to tell me about myself, to tell me about Echo Company, and to tell me who was really in charge. You know, when you are flying around in a helicopter in Vietnam you don't really know where you are until you make the place by landing. I want to know who is in charge and I want to figure out how to put the dreams away.

I have never stopped fighting even since I came home. It seems that's all I do. I am still sleeping with a forty-five, even though I know there is no bogeyman coming to get me. I can't stand being on an airplane because I don't like confined spaces. I first got claustrophobia in Vietnam, not in a confined space, but in a paddy field. There was no way to get out. You just had to serve your time.

I am extremely bitter, and it's getting worse year by year. It's got me worried, my fatalism is becoming dominant and he's a hard guy to deal with. There was a time I almost shot myself and my wife because I wanted to do her a favor. I am completely unrestricted and I'm bored to death. Let's not think that we are the only ones who are wounded by Vietnam, you only have to look at the yuppies to see people who are victims of emotional numbing.

I know there are no enemies on the memorial, just names—it's perfectly safe. When I got close to it, I just got angry. But from a distance, it's gray and I can't see the names and I don't feel angry. If you do the American hero, you get the American dream, and the American dream is simply this: fear of the future.

I'll tell you one thing, my enemy would respect me more than my own country, and what is this, are we all pardoned now? That's what I would have put here, a big pardon for the Vietnam veteran. Something that says, "Sorry, boys."

LLOYD WOLF, an award-winning photographer, was recently honored by *Washingtonian* magazine as one of the ten best photographers in the Washington, D.C., area.

DUNCAN SPENCER, a writer and former *Washington Star* reporter, is a graduate of Yale University.